the beacon rec

(Revised Edition)

MW01686685

Book Two: Part 2

Little Chick-Chick

By **James H. Fassett**

Series Editor (Revised Edition)
Francis Fanthome

Ginn

Revised Edition 2002
EOU Printing 2009

Illustrations: Jatandeep Singh
Layout and design: Textsure
Printed by Pearson Education Asia LTD.

(CTPS/02)

USING THIS BOOK

This, the second of the two main readers for the Book Two Stage of Beacon Reading, contains more of the old, much-loved nursery tales which are part of the child's inheritance. The cumulative character of these stories provides in an exciting setting the repetition necessary for word mastery and builds up the child's confidence in his ability to read.

The preparation for reading each story in this book is essential for its fullest enjoyment and use. This preparation should consist of (a) revision of sight words learnt in the previous stages and again occurring in the story (see below), (b) teaching the new sight words listed at the head of the story. In the daily and separate phonic period, revision, based on the tables on pp.54 and 55, should go hand in hand with the teaching of the new phonic groups on pages 56-59. It is most important that the new phonic work in each of the Phonic Group Tables XXIII-XXXIII should be thoroughly familiar to the child before he applies it to his reading.

NEW WORDS USED IN THIS BOOK

Of the 148 words the children should have learned to pronounce and recognize the 114 in italics through their previous phonic training. Each of the 34 new sight words is shown at the head of the story in which it first appears and the children should be able to recognize it before reading the story.

SIGHT WORDS NEEDED

are	farmer	horse	no	so	what
be	found	house	O	some	where
come	give	I	of	the	who
could	go	little	oh	they	wolf
cow	going	me	old	to	would
do	good	Mr.	one	two	you
don't	have	Mrs.	other	very	your
down	he	more	said	was	
ears	her	mother	she	water	

CONTENTS

LITTLE CHICK-CHICK

acorn choking fast cobbler
leather pair after

One day Little Chick-Chick found a dry acorn.
Mother Hen said to her,
"Chick-Chick, you must not eat that dry acorn.
It will make you choke, choke, in your little throat, throat."
Little Chick-Chick said,
"O Mother, I am so big that I can eat an acorn."
But the little acorn did make her choke, choke in her little throat, throat.

New words: acorn *choke* *throat*

So Mother Hen ran to the pond.

And Mother Hen said,

"O Pond, give me some water, for Little Chick-Chick is choking."

But the pond said to her,

"You must get the old oak tree to give you a cup.

Then I can give you some water for Little Chick-Chick."

Mother Hen ran to the oak tree.

New words: choking *oak*

And Mother Hen said,

"Tree, Tree, do give me a cup, so that Pond can give me water, for Little Chick-Chick is choking."

The old oak tree said to her,

"You must get Man to shake me.

Then I can give you a cup."

Mother Hen ran to the man.

And Mother Hen said to him,

"Man, Man, shake Oak Tree.

New words: *shake*

Then Oak Tree will give me a cup, and I will take it to Pond, so that Pond can give me water, for Little Chick-Chick is choking."

But the man said to her,

"You must get the cobbler to make me some new boots.

Then I will shake the oak tree."

Mother Hen ran as fast as she could to the cobbler.

And Mother Hen said to him,

"O Cobbler, Cobbler, please make me some boots.

New words: boots cobbler fast *new*

Then Man will shake Oak Tree.

And Oak Tree will give me a cup, so that Pond can give me water, for Little Chick-Chick is choking."

But the cobbler said to her,

"You must first get the cow, to give me some leather.

Then I can make you the boots."

New words: *first* leather

Mother Hen ran to the cow.

And Mother Hen said,

"O Cow, will you please give me some leather?

Then Cobbler will make me some boots.

And Man will shake Oak Tree.

Oak Tree will give me a cup, so that Pond can give me water, for Little Chick-Chick is choking."

But the cow said to her,

"You must first get the farmer to give me some grain.

Then I will give you leather for the new boots."

Mother Hen ran to the farmer.

New words: *grain*

And Mother Hen said,

"Farmer, give me some grain.

Then the cow will give me some leather.

And Cobbler will make me some boots.

And Man will shake Oak Tree.

Then the Oak tree will give me a cup, so that Pond can give me water, for Little Chick-Chick is choking."

The good farmer said to her,

"Yes, I will give you some of my grain."

Then Mother Hen ran to give the grain to the cow.

The cow gave her some leather.

Mother Hen gave the Leather to the cobbler.

Then the cobbler made for her a fine new pair of boots.

Mother Hen gave the new boots to the man.

He gave Oak Tree a shake.

New words: pair

Then Oak Tree gave Mother Hen a clean little cup.

The pond gave her some water.

Mother Hen gave the cup of water to Little Chick-Chick.

So the acorn did not choke Little Chick-Chick after all.

New words: after

IF ALL THE SEAS

great were

If all the seas were one sea,
What a great sea that would be!
If all the trees were one tree,
What a great tree that would be!
And if a man cut down the tree
And let it fall into the sea,
What a splish, splash that would be!

New words: great sea seas splash splish were

HUMPTY DUMPTY

again

Humpty Dumpty sat on a wall.
Humpty Dumpty had a great fall.
Not all the king's horses,
Nor all the king's men,
Could set Humpty Dumpty up again.

New words: again Dumpty horses Humpty king's men nor sat wall

THE LITTLE FIR TREE

gold glass along

In a grove of all oaks was one little fir tree.

It was a pretty little tree, but it felt sad. One day it said,

"I do wish I had green leaves.

All the other trees have leaves.

My needles are hard and stiff.

The birds will not nest in them."

New words: *birds felt fir green grove hard leaves needles nest oaks sad stiff tall*

Next day, when the little tree woke up, it had green leaves.

It was just like the other trees.

"Now I am happy," it said.

But a goat came along and ate all the green leaves.

"Oh, dear!" said the fir tree.

"I wish I had gold leaves.

Goats do not eat gold leaves."

Next day, when the little tree woke up, it had gold leaves.

"How happy I am!" it said.

New words: goat goats gold happy now woke

But a man came along and stole all the gold leaves.

"Oh, dear!" said the fir tree.

"I wish I had glass leaves.

Men do not steal glass leaves."

Next day, when the little tree woke up, it had glass leaves.

"How happy I am!" it said.

"See my leaves shine in the sun."

But a strong wind sprang up.

"Woo-oo!" said the wind.

And it broke all the glass leaves.

New words: along glass *shine* *sprang* *steal* *stole* *strong* *wind* *woo-oo*

"Oh, dear!" said the fir tree.

"I wish I had my needles again.

Goats do not eat them.

No one will steal them.

The wind will do them no harm."

Then the tree went to sleep.

When it woke up the next day it had all its needles again.

"Oh, I never was so happy!" said the little fir tree.

New words: *broke* *harm* *its* *never* *sleep*

THE LAMBKIN

grow iron roll there

last rolled door called

Lambkin said, "I am so thin that I am just skin and bone.

I have not had a thing to eat for a long time. I will skip and run till I come to Granny's house.

Granny will give me all sorts of good things to eat."

So Lambkin went skip, skip, skipping along to Granny's house.

New words: *granny's* lambkin *long* *skin* *skip* *skipping* *sorts* *thing*

On the way he met Mr. Fox.

Mr. Fox said, "Stop, Lambkin! I am going to eat you up."

But Lambkin said to him,

"To Granny's house I go,
Where I shall fatter grow,
Then you can eat me so."

"You may go," said Mr. Fox.

"You are such a thin little chap that you are just skin and bone."

So Lambkin went skip, skip, skipping along to Granny's house.

New words: *chap fatter fox grow stop such way*

On the way he met Mr. Wolf.

Mr. Wolf said, "Stop, Lambkin! I am going to eat you up."

But Lambkin said to him,

"To Granny's house I go,
Where I shall fatter grow,
Then you can eat me so."

"You may go," said Mr. Wolf.

"You are such a thin little chap that you are just skin and bone."

So Lambkin went skip, skip, skipping along to Granny's house.

On the way he met Mr. Lion.

Mr. Lion said, "Stop, Lambkin! I am going to eat you up."

But Lambkin said to him,

"To Granny's house I go,
Where I shall fatter grow,
Then you can eat me so."

"You may go," said Mr. Lion.

"You are such a thin little chap that you are just skin and bone."

So Lambkin went skip, skip, skipping along to Granny's house.

New words: lion

Lambkin said to Granny, "O Granny, please give me lots of good things to eat so that I shall grow fat."

So Granny gave Lambkin all sorts of good things to eat — apples and sweets and nuts and figs and cake and jam.

Lambkin began to grow fatter and fatter and fatter.

Then he said to Granny, "Please make me a drumkin that will roll, and then I will get into it and go home."

New words: drumkin granny lots nuts roll sweets

So Granny made a drumkin.

When Lambkin got into it the drumkin began to roll and roll.

"I shall soon be there," said Lambkin.

On the way they met Mr. Lion.

"Have you seen Lambkin?" said Mr. Lion.

Lambkin in the drumkin said,

"Tum-pa-too, tum-pa-too,
Lambkin's lost, and so are you."

Drumkin began to roll and roll.

New words: *lambkin's* *seen* *soon* there *tum-pa-too*

On the way they met Mr. Wolf.

"Have you seen Lambkin?" said Mr. Wolf.

Lambkin in the drumkin said,

"Tum-pa-too, tum-pa-too,
Lambkin's lost, and so are you."

Drumkin began to roll and roll.

On the way they met Mr. Fox.

"Have you seen Lambkin?" said Mr. Fox.

Lambkin in the drumkin said,

"Tum-pa-too, tum-pa-too,
Lambkin's lost, and so are you."

But Mr. Fox said to himself, "What can this mean?

A drumkin can not speak, and so I think Lambkin must be in the drumkin."

Then the drumkin began to roll.

And Mr. Fox began to run.

New words: *himself* *mean* *speak*

Faster and faster they went.

At last the drumkin rolled up to the door of Lambkin's house.

Lambkin gave one jump out of the drumkin into the house.

Then he shut the door.

He called out to Mr. Fox,

"When you catch Drumkin you may eat Lambkin.

Good-bye, Mr. Fox!"

New words: called door *faster* last rolled *shut*

IN BED

"I see the moon,

and the moon sees me.

God bless the moon,

and God bless me."

The little girl is in bed.

She is not ready to go to sleep.

She sees the new moon.

The new moon is not round.

It has two sharp tips.

It is like a boat.

New words: *bless* *boat* *girl* *God* *moon* *round* *sees* *sharp* *tips*

A BOY AND AN OWL

flew

A little boy went into a barn
And lay down on some hay;
An owl came out and flew about,
And the little boy ran away.

New words: *about* *barn* *boy* *flew* *lay* *owl*

FUNNY BUNNY RABBIT

cabbage soup baa-baa

One day Funny Bunny Rabbit found a cabbage, and she said,

"The cabbage will make me some good soup."

So Funny Bunny Rabbit cut the cabbage.

She went hop-pi-ty-hop, till she came to her little house.

But she could not get in.

New words: *bunny* cabbage soup

"Who is in my little house?" said Funny Bunny Rabbit.

And a loud voice said,

"I am big Mr. Goat,
I am in here to stay,
I shall eat you all up,
If you don't go away."

So Funny Bunny Rabbit went hop-pi-ty-hop, hop-pi-ty-hop, till she met Mr. Pig.

New words: *hop-pi-ty-hop* *loud* *stay* *voice*

And she said to him,

"O Mr. Pig, I found a cabbage, a cabbage good for soup.

I ran to my house.

I could not get in.

A loud voice said,

'I am big Mr. Goat,
I am in here to stay,
I shall eat you all up,
If you don't go away.'

Please help me, Mr. Pig!"

But Mr. Pig said,

"I cannot help you.

I am afraid of Old Mr. Goat".

So Funny Bunny Rabbit went hop-pi-ty-hop, hop-pi-ty-hop, till she met Mrs. Cow.

And she said to her,

"O Mrs. Cow, I found a cabbage,

a cabbage good for soup.

I ran to my house.

I could not get in.

A loud voice said,

'I am big Mr. Goat,
I am in here to stay,
I shall eat you all up,
If you don't go away.'

Please help me, do help me, good Mrs. Cow."

But Mrs. Cow said, "I cannot help you.

I am afraid of Old Mr. Goat."

So Funny Bunny Rabbit went hop-pi-ty-hop, hop-pi-ty-hop, till she met Mr. Dog.

"O Mr. Dog, I found a cabbage, a cabbage good for soup.

I ran to my house.

I could not get in.

A loud voice said,

'I am big Mr. Goat,
I am in here to stay,
I shall eat you all up,
If you don't go away.'

Please help me, do help me, good Mr. Dog."

But Mr. Dog said, "I can not help you.

I am afraid of Old Mr. Goat."

So Funny Bunny Rabbit went hop-pi-ty-hop, hop-pi-ty-hop, till she met Little Bee.

"O Little Bee, I found a cabbage, a cabbage good for soup.

I ran to my house.

I could not get in.

A loud voice said,

'I am big Mr. Goat,
I am in here to stay,
I shall eat you all up,
If you don't go away'.

The pig cannot help me.

The cow cannot help me.

New words: *bee*

The dog cannot help me.
And you cannot help me.
You are so very little."
But the little bee said, "Let me see this old goat.
I may be little, but I can help you."
So Funny Bunny Rabbit went to her house again.
And Little Bee went with her.
Funny Bunny Rabbit said, "Go away, Old Mr. Goat.
This is my little house."

But the old goat said,

"I am big Mr. Goat,
I am in here to stay,
I shall eat you all up,
If you don't go away."

Then the little bee flew and flew and flew.

She flew down the chimney.
She stung Big Mr. Goat.
She stung him on the nose.
She stung him on the ears.
She stung him on the tail.

New words: *chimney* *stung*

Then Big Mr. Goat said, "Baa-baa-baa-baa!"
And Big Mr. Goat ran away.
He ran and he ran and he ran.

And Funny Bunny Rabbit went into her little house.

She set some water on the boil and made some cabbage soup.

New words: baa-baa *boil*

THE THREE LITTLE PIGS

lived poor pair blow

huffed puffed blew burned

An old mother pig and her three little pigs
lived in a very small house.
One day Old Mother Pig said,
"This house is too small for us.
Little Pigs, you must go away.
You must each make a house."

New words: *each* lived *pigs* *small*

So the first little pig went away to make a house.

He met a man with some straw.

The little pig said to the man,

"Mr. Man, please sell me some straw to make a house."

And the man said to him,

"Why, you poor little pig!

I will give you all the straw you need to make a house."

New words: poor *sell* *why*

So the little pig made a house out of straw.
He was very happy in it.

Then Old Mr. Wolf came along.
He went up to the little house of straw, and said,

"Little pig, little pig,
Let me in, let me in."

But the little pig said,
"No, no, by the hair
Of my chinny-chin-chin,
I will not let you in."
And the old wolf said,
"Then I'll huff and I'll puff,
And I'll blow your house in."
So he huffed and he puffed
And he blew the house in.
And he ate up the poor little pig.

New words: blew blow *chinny-chin* hair *huff* huffed *puff* puffed

Then the next little pig went away to make a new house.

He met a man with some sticks.

And he said to the man, "Please, sir, will you sell me a few sticks to make a house?"

And the man said, "Why, you poor little pig!

I will give you all the sticks you need to make a house."

So the little pig made a house for himself out of sticks.

New words: *few* *sir*

Then Old Mr. Wolf came along.

He went up to the little house made of sticks, and said,

"Little pig, little pig,
Let me in, let me in."

But the little pig said,

"No, no, by the hair
Of my chinny-chin-chin,
I will not let you in."

And Old Mr. Wolf said,

"Then I'll huff and I'll puff,
And I'll blow your house in."

So he huffed and he puffed
And he blew the house in.
And he ate up the poor little pig.

Then the third little pig went away to make himself a house.

He met a man with some bricks.

And he said to the man,

"Please, Mr. Man, will you sell me a few of your bricks so that I may make a house?"

New words: *third*

And the man said,

"Why, you poor little pig!

I will give you all the bricks you need to make a house."

So the little pig made a house for himself out of bricks.

Then Old Mr. Wolf came along

He went up to the little house made of bricks and said

"Little pig, little pig,
Let me in, let me in."

But the little pig said,

"No, no, by the hair
Of my chinny-chin-chin,
I will not let you in."

And the old wolf said,

"Then I'll huff and I'll puff,
And I'll blow your house in."

So he huffed and he puffed,
And he puffed and he huffed,
But he could not blow in the house made of bricks.

Then Old Mr. Wolf said,
"I will go down the chimney.
Then I will eat you up."

New words: *couldn't*

But Little Pig made a big fire.

When the old wolf came down the chimney, Little Pig said,

"Fire, Fire, burn Wolf!"

So the fire began to burn, and it burned and it burned, till it burned up Mr. Wolf.

And that was the end of him.

NOTE ON BEACON PHONICS

The phonic group tables overleaf continue without a break the phonic work which accompanied the reading of *Old Dog Tom*. When the work on these tables has been completed the child will have the key to the pronunciation and recognition of ninety-six per cent of the words that he will ever meet in his reading.

Because it is a fundamental Beacon principle that new phonic steps should be introduced and well practised before the child is asked to apply them in his reading, it is most important that the work provided by a particular Group Table should be completed during the period defined in the note at the head of the table. Only if the phonic work is dealt with in this way can teacher and child experience the happiness and sense of progress, the freedom from drudgery, and the quick passage from one page of the reader to the next, which result from preparation well and truly made.

Revision of work previously done should always form part of the daily phonic period.

PHONIC GROUP TABLES

Revision table for Groups VI-IX (see *At Home*).

chap	such	shut	cracks
cock	bricks	dress	pitch
think	smell	felt	things
king	skin	thing	back
lots	nuts	when	trot
milk	went	lift	drink
sticks	skip	bless	must
	splish, splash	huff-puff	

Revision table for Groups X-XVI (see *At Play*).

fox	please	bone	lean
shine	woke	sweets	plain
meat	beans	beef	sleep
hay	way	stay	make
peas	tea	each	mean
takes	vain	yes	yeast
choke	buzz	wife	make
ears	quick	three	side
grove	leaves	duke	teeth

Revision table for Groups XVII-XXII (see *Old Dog Tom*).

roast	goes	road	toes
straw	paws	mew	tied
throat	oak	boots	new
goat	goats	oaks	wall
all	dawn	pool	drawn
boom	roost	small	pool

fly	dry	dries	dried
die	cry	pie	good
dies	cries	pies	hoop
died	cried	cook	look
draw	book	cure	due
shoot	mule	tune	hall

shawl	stew	stall	tubes
boat	moon	news	fault
my	toad	Paul	call
mew	soon	few	hood
fall	shook	broom	tries
stool	loaf	loaves	claw

Group XXIII. Words containing the vowel *o* modified by *r*. For application see p.5 onward.

horn	nor	north	sorts
torn	short	for	fork
corn	storm	cord	born

Group XXIV. Words containing the vowel *a* modified by *r*. For application see p.10 onward.

hard	harm	sharp	barn
farms	tarts	part	dark
star	charm	car	park

Group XXV. Words containing the vowel *e, i, u,* modified by *r*. For application see p.10 onward.

first	her	burn	burns
jerk	birds	fir	stern
burnt	perch	turn	shirt

Revision table for *Groups XXIII-XXV*

port	cart	car	corn
dirt	horn	hurt	fern
stir	spark	stork	turn
kerb	term	third	purr
thirst	churn	barks	term
hard	hers	burnt	skirt

Group XXVI. Two-syllable words ending in *y* or *ey* with the short sound of *i*. For application see p.15 onward.

dolly	happy	funny
stormy	dirty	granny
puppy	candy	kitty
kidney	donkey	curly
turkey	jersey	jockey
Charley	chimney	valley

Humpty Dumpty chinny-chin

marry	sorry	hurry
merry	tarry	sherry
berry	Harry	scurry
carry	ferry	lorry

Group XXVII. Two-syllable words ending in *le*. For application see p.16 onward.

little	apples	bubble
steeple	tumble	candle
kettle	battle	cackle
needles	bottle	settle
thimble	middle	jingle
crumple	eagle	riddle
muddle	nibble	scramble

Group XXVIII. Words in which *ou* and *ow* have the sound as in *cow*. For application see p.17 onward.

cows	out	pout	mouse
now	our	found	house
how	sour	round	drown
bows	owls	mouth	bound
loud	down	towns	sound

Group XXIX. Some common two-syllable words. For application see p.20 onward.

ticket	platter	singing
pocket	matter	ringing
bucket	copper	banging
packet	stammer	drawing
rabbit	corner	rocking
sandpit	bitter	sticking
titbit	farmer	hopping
dig	shop	hunt
digger	shopper	hunter
digging	shopping	hunting
farm	skip	run
farmer	skipper	runner
farming	skipping	running

Group XXX. Words containing the obscure sound of initial *a*. For application see p.30 onward.

away	afraid	alone	amuse
agree	awake	asleep	alike
alarm	ajar	across	about
ablaze	abed	along	alive

Revision tables for Groups XXIII-XXX.

for	far	birds	turns
hard	horn	funny	her
house	out	along	how
alive	our	round	now
first	tarts	bunny	tower
howl	part	short	towns
drops	burn	proud	frown

Sally	car	happy	third
Charley	barn	sorry	stern
Dora	fern	merry	eagle
Harry	cord	hurry	eager
Vicky	born	berry	claws
Nanny	torn	carry	about
Teddy	fear	curry	across

Revision table for Groups XXIII-XXX (*contd.*)

middle	puffing	dropping
number	sweeter	howling
around	swinging	sprinkle
pocket	dropper	burning
bonnet	dangle	clawing
spangle	flower	running
slumber	dipping	sunny
across	rabbit	asleep
corner	bigger	fatter
donkey	stormy	turkey
porter	amouse	aloud
wheeling	farmer	platter
needles	skipping	cobbler

Group XXXI. Words in which *oi* and *oy* are pronounced as in *boy*. For application see p.30 onward.

boy	oil	soil	point
toys	coil	toils	spoil
joy	boil	foil	noise
enjoy	coin	annoy	joint

employ joining boiling

Group XXXII. Words in which *c* before *e* is pronounced like *s*. For application see p.32 onward.

ace	place	race	ice
mice	voice	dance	trace
fence	cease	nice	twice
slice	price	spice	lace
face	rice	pace	dice

Revision table for various groups.

dry	sail	thorn	growl
boy	voice	loud	barn
about	flew	little	away
funny	house	near	stay
found	afraid	made	small
first	straw	bricks	sticks

market	puffing	huffing
pointing	soiling	spoiling

Group XXXIII. Words in which *g* and *dg* before *e* have the sound of *j*. Notice that *dge* is used after a short vowel. For application see *The Pancake* (Book Three Stage of Beacon Reading).

age	bridge	rage	ridge
edge	wage	ledge	nudge
judge	badge	stage	page
large	cage	huge	lodge

Revision tables in which are included all phonic words met for the first time in the reading matter of *Old Dog Tom* and *Little Chick-Chick*.

back	bit	puff	gave
cracks	milk	huff	ate
flap	skip	muffins	make
Ann	till	made	buns
grand	tip	tail	sun

chap	dinner	cut	hay
sad	sticks	stung	plain
pet	Tom	such	vain
met	along	shuts	takes
egg	trot	bunny	may
left	lots	funny	shake
when	fox	nuts	grain
bless	God	p-r-r	days
sell	stop	burn	stay
went	long	first	way
next	toss	third	lay
felt	song	girl	away

drumkin	Humpty Dumpty
skipping	hoppity-hop
tum-pa-too	splish, splash

Revision table (*contd.*)

afraid	bone	never	bill
about	roast	nest	lift
began	goes	smell	stiff
between	road	set	pitch
begins	toes	press	dress
belong	nose	men	think
wife	choke	wings	its
dry	stole	bricks	that
quite	throat	king's	that's
reply	oak	skin	fish
why	boat	things	strong
side	oaks	tips	sharp
tied	grove	thing	grand
shine	goat	himself	sprang
fire	goats	wind	fatter
by	woke	pigs	rabbit
my	broke	bring	happy
mice	home	gift	granny

burning	granny's	rooster's
wheeling	rooster	chimney

Revision tables (*contd.*)

fir	paws	mean	beef
birds	tall	lean	clean
cart	small	meat	sweet
barn	cook	steal	sweet
hard	book	peas	leaves
sharp	look	please	boy
harm	boots	bee	voice
sorts	soon	seen	boil
nor	moon	sees	out
sir	looks	need	owl
mew	tea	three	drown
new	teeth	sleep	mouth
few	sea	green	cow
straw	seas	sleep	round
call	each	speak	loud
wall	ears	beans	now

cobbler	himself	platter
horses	needles	farmer
chinny-chin-chin		faster
cock-a-doodle-doo		woo-oo

EXERCISES

1. Why did Mother Hen tell Chick-Chick not to eat the acorn?

2. Why was the little fir tree sad?

3. What did Lambkin say to Mr. Fox when he met him on the way to Granny's?

4. What does the little girl in bed see?

5. What did Funny Bunny Rabbit find on the way? What did she want to do with it?

6. Who was in Funny Bunny Rabbit's house and what did the loud voice say?

7. How did the little bee help Funny Bunny Rabbit?

8. What did the first little pig make his house of?

9. What did the wolf say to the three little pigs?

10. How did Mr. Wolf meet his end?

11. Write five new words you have learnt in this book and five words learnt from the earlier books.